WEIRD WEATHER

by **Clare Oliver**

Contents

Clever Clogs Books
Copyright © 2006 *ticktock* Entertainment Ltd.
http://www.ticktock.co.uk

SUN SACRIFICES

Energy from the Sun is the source of all life on this planet. Many early civilisations worshipped the Sun. High on their pyramid-shaped temples, Aztec priests made grisly human sacrifices to their god of sun and rain, Tlaloc.

Tlaloc

POLE POWER

Chief of all the spirits worshipped by the Native Americans was the Thunderbird. Tribes often built tall totem poles in the bird's honour. Lightning was said to shoot from its beak and thunder to roll from its beating wings. But, most importantly, the Thunderbird brought refreshing rain to water the Earth and make the plants grow.

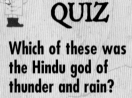

WEATHER QUIZ

Which of these was the Hindu god of thunder and rain?

a) Zeus
b) Thor
c) Indra

Who was the Mayan god of storms?

a) Galan
b) Huracan
c) Blusteran

Which musical instrument is used in raindance ceremonies?

a) xylophone
b) synthesiser
c) bullroarer

(answers on page 32)

SPRINGING A LEAK

The Chippewa Indians of North America told a story to help them explain springtime flooding. According to legend, the Sun's heat was held in a bag during the winter. But each spring a mouse nibbled a hole in the bag. All the heat leaked out, melting the snow on the mountain tops and causing floods.

DIVINE INTERVENTION

Weather has such awesome power it's no wonder some people in the past blamed, or thanked, their gods for it. Until we worked out what caused it, extreme weather must sometimes have seemed like the end of the world. People relied on fine sunny days and sprinklings of rain to ripen and water their crops.

Thunderbird totem pole

BUSY BEETLE

Ancient Egyptians thought a dung beetle, known as a scarab, pushed their sun god Re across the sky every day.

SONG & DANCE

In times of drought, special rituals are sometimes performed to bring on the rain. African rain magic included dancing, chanting, sprinkling small amounts of precious water – and even spitting!

STRANGE FOREBODINGS

Some people rely on the feel of their boots to decide whether to carry an umbrella or not. Others base their forecasts on the behaviour of plants or animals. Do natural signs give us clues to the weather? You decide.

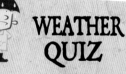

WEATHER QUIZ

When do grass-hoppers get noisier?

a) when they are arguing
b) when snow is forecast
c) as the temperature rises

Why do people hang seaweed on their garden walls?

a) to forecast the weather
b) they think it looks pretty
c) the smell puts off burglars

When do shepherds and sailors like to see a red sky?

a) at night
b) in the morning
c) on 4 July

(answers on page 32)

FIR-LY ACCURATE

Pine cones are surprisingly sensitive to weather. When it is dry, their scales shrivel and open out. When rain is on the way, their scales absorb moisture from the air and close up. Flowers also react to the weather. Dandelions snap shut if the temperature drops below 10°C, while the delicate scarlet pimpernel's petals close just before it rains.

Open pine cone, dry weather

MOO-VE IT!

People say cows lie down when it is going to rain so that they will have somewhere dry to sit out the storm. Problem is, cows are not the brightest of creatures. They are just as likely to lie down when there are only clear skies on the horizon!

4

WEATHER CALENDAR

Whatever the weather on St Swithin's Day (15 July), it is said that 40 more days of the same will follow. This is because Swithin, bishop of Winchester, unleashed a torrential, 40-day rainstorm on 15 July 971. He was dead at the time but he had got uppity when his remains were moved against his wishes.

ME & MY SHADOW

If the groundhog sees its own shadow when it wakes up from its winter sleep, people must expect six more weeks of wintry weather.

WAKE-UP, WOODCHUCK!

Groundhog Day is celebrated in the United States on 2 February when revellers watch what the groundhog does as it wakes. Also known as woodchucks, some of these small furry creatures are celebrities – Philadelphia's most famous, Punxsutawney Phil, even featured in a film.

A cow expecting rain?

COTTONWOOL CLOUDS

Clouds are one of the most beautiful features of the sky. From space, you can see huge white wisps constantly swirling above the Earth. These massive collections of cold water or ice may look like fluffy cottonwool, but they're far from soft to the touch.

Earth from space

WET BLANKET

Every cloud is made up of billions of tiny water droplets or ice crystals. Warm air cools as it rises, which causes the moisture in it to condense into microscopic droplets of water. Clouds that form very high in the sky – where the air is so cold it's freezing – form snow clouds packed with ice crystals.

HEAD IN THE CLOUDS

Maybe no two clouds look alike to you, but scientists say clouds come in ten basic kinds and three shapes. In 1803, Luke Howard was the first person to sort the clouds into different types. This budding English scientist must have paid attention in school, because all the cloud names he came up with were in Latin.

CLOUD CALL

Cumulonimbus

When you look up at the sky, you will see different types of cloud. High, wispy clouds are called cirrus, after the Latin for 'curl of hair'. Cumulus clouds are the classic, intensely white cottonwool clouds. Their name means 'heap'. Stratus clouds are flat, layered clouds. But the ones to watch out for are nimbus clouds – they bring rain!

The world's **RAIN AGAIN** rainiest place is in Hawaii. Expect to need a brolly on Mount Wai-'ale-'ale for all but two weeks of the year.

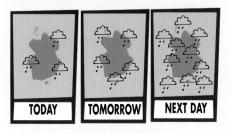

| TODAY | TOMORROW | NEXT DAY |

MIX & MATCH

Weather watchers today can go even further to describe clouds. The idea is to combine different words and come up with a perfect description for every clouds. So a cumulonimbus cloud is a large, fluffy cloud that brings rain. Putting 'cirro-' or 'alto-' in front of the cloud describes whether it is a high-level or mid-level cloud. Try mixing and matching your own!

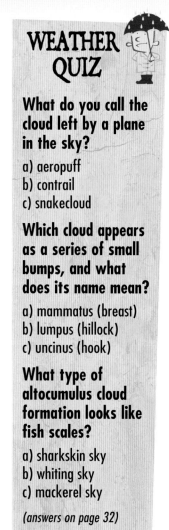

WEATHER QUIZ

What do you call the cloud left by a plane in the sky?

a) aeropuff
b) contrail
c) snakecloud

Which cloud appears as a series of small bumps, and what does its name mean?

a) mammatus (breast)
b) lumpus (hillock)
c) uncinus (hook)

What type of altocumulus cloud formation looks like fish scales?

a) sharkskin sky
b) whiting sky
c) mackerel sky

(answers on page 32)

Magnified ice crystals

FANTASTIC FLAKES

Next time you catch a snowflake on your mitt, have a close look at it. Every snowflake is six-sided and made up of microscopic ice crystals, but that's where the similarities end. In fact, every snowflake is as unique as each of your fingerprints. No one has ever seen two flakes that look the same.

WEATHER QUIZ

Which night-time visitor is said to bring frost?

a) Jack Frost
b) Jane Frost
c) Frosty the Snowman

How much of fresh snow is made up of air?

a) over 90 per cent
b) 50 per cent
c) there is no air; it is only made of water

Which ship sank when it hit an iceberg?

a) the _Gigantic_
b) the _Titanic_
c) the _Unsinkable_

(answers on page 32)

HAIL & HEAVY

The biggest ever hailstones hit Gopalganj in Bangladesh in April 1996. Each one weighed more than 1 kg – ouch!

THE BIG FREEZE

Believe it or not, we live in a warm period in Earth's history. Climate boffins say we are in the Holocene Epoch. They reckon this period began about 10,000 years ago when we were still living in caves. Before that was the Pleistocene Epoch that included about seven ice ages – times when at least a third of the Earth was covered in moving sheets of ice.

WINTER WONDERLAND

Frost's pretty cool, but you can't beat waking up to a thick blanket of fresh snow. It's like waking up in a new world where there is a ready supply of missiles to throw and snowy sculptures to create. Now THAT's cool!

Snowman

CHILL OUT

Of course, the snowiest, coldest places on Earth are the North and South Poles. Ice there never really melts, except for around the coast. New snow just falls on top of the old, pressing it down into superthick sheets of ice. In parts of Antarctica the ice has never once melted in over two million years!

MONSTER MELTDOWN?

Even today there are tens of thousands of glaciers, mostly around Antarctica and Greenland. If all the frozen water locked up in these glaciers melted at once, the sea would rise by about 60 metres. Every major coastal city – including New York and Sydney – would disappear!

WHITE OUT

Serious winter weather can bring serious danger. Biting blizzards trap people in their own homes. Power cables collapse under the weight of the snowfall, leaving many people without heating or electricity. And in remote mountain areas the sheer weight of snow can send terrifying avalanches tumbling down.

AVALANCHE!

Avalanches happen after sudden, heavy snow, or in spring when the winter snows begin to melt. A sudden movement or noise, such as a car engine backfiring, dislodges the snow or ice and sets it moving. The avalanche rapidly gathers speed and can thunder down the mountainside at over 320 km/h.

WALL OF DEATH

If you find yourself in the path of a thundering wall of ice and snow, don't expect to survive. If the sheer weight of impact doesn't get you, the freezing conditions soon will. After 20 minutes, 70 per cent of avalanche victims have usually died.

After an avalanche

BANG! BANG!

During the Second World War, about 60,000 men died in the Tyrolean Alps – not from enemy gunfire, but from avalanches set off by the sound of gunshots.

LICK OF LIFE

The most heroic dog of all time was a St Bernard called Barry. He saved more than 40 people in the Swiss Alps. He once rescued a boy who lay under an avalanche next to his mother's dead body. Barry gently licked the boy's face until he woke up, then carried him to safety.

Rescue team

MOUNTAIN MUTTS

Dogs speed up the rescue work. Their noses can sniff out people – even if they're buried beneath metres of snow. In a couple of hours, a pair of dogs can cover the same area as 80 human rescuers!

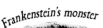

Lightning strikes the Earth 100 times every second.

FAR OUT

Check out your chances of being stuck in an electrical storm. Light travels faster than sound, so count the seconds between a lightning flash and its thunder clap. Every three seconds equals about 1 km between you and the storm. If you see lightning and hear thunder at the same time, you're in trouble!

Lightning over Arizona, USA

Frankenstein's monster

MONSTER FORCE

In the eighteenth century, some people believed electricity was the life force that made human bodies work. In Mary Shelley's famous horror story, Dr Frankenstein sparks his freaky monster to life by harnessing electricity from a storm. We might take electricity for granted but scientists who experimented with it in the early days would have been shocked to see the amazing machines and gadgets it powers for us.

THUNDERBOLTS & LIGHTNING...

Very, very frightening! What's more, there are about 40,000 thunderstorms on Earth every day!

CHARGING ABOUT

As so much heat rises in the air on a hot day it provides perfect conditions for dark storm clouds to brew. Drops of water jiggle around inside the cumulonimbus cloud and it is soon crackling with electricity. Lightning flashes are charges of static electricity that are attracted either down to the ground or across the sky to another cloud.

ELECTRI-FRIED!

Roy Sullivan, a park ranger in Virginia, United States, was struck by lightning seven times between 1942 and 1977. Over the years, he lost a toenail and suffered burns to his legs, stomach, chest and left shoulder. His eyebrows burnt off in 1969 and his hair went up in flames – twice!

WEATHER QUIZ

Why is it a bad idea to shelter under a tree in a thunderstorm?

a) you might frighten away small animals
b) leaves direct rain down the back of your neck
c) lightning usually strikes tall objects

How often does lightning strike the Empire State Building in New York City?

a) 5 times a year
b) 20 times a year
c) 500 times a year

Which US President flew a kite in a thunderstorm?

a) Benjamin Franklin
b) Abraham Lincoln
c) Bill Clinton

(answers on page 32)

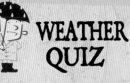

WEATHER QUIZ

What name is given to the still centre of a hurricane?

a) eye
b) pie
c) sky

How fast must a wind be before it's called a hurricane?

a) more than 89 km/h
b) more than 119 km/h
c) more than 229 km/h

What is a storm surge?

a) a swell of seawater just before a hurricane
b) an extra-powerful gust of wind
c) a doctor who treats hurricane victims

(answers on page 32)

The Superdome in New Orleans

Katastrophic Katrina

In September 2005, Hurricane Katrina devastated the southern US city of New Orleans. At the peak of its power, the wind speed was approximately 200 km/h. Extensive floods led to the mass evacuation of the city and nearby towns, and residents and tourists had to seek shelter in the Superdome after 80 per cent of the city sunk below sea level after defensive barriers were overwhelmed.

THE NAME GAME

An Australian weather expert called Clement Wragge had the idea of naming tropical storms in the nineteenth century. He chose boys' names from the Bible, such as Rakem and Talmon. Since 1978, hurricanes have alternately been given a boy or girl's name.

IN A SPIN

Hurricanes south of the equator spin clockwise. In the north, they whirl in the opposite direction – anti-clockwise!

14

HURRICANE HELL

The world's most terrifying storms are hurricanes. Whirling winds race along at up to 360 km/h, carrying swirling thunderclouds and torrential rain. Every second, a hurricane generates ten times more energy than the atom bomb that was dropped on Hiroshima, Japan, in the Second World War.

TROPICAL TROUBLE

Terrifying tropical storms sink ships, batter coastlines and flatten houses. They are known variously as hurricanes over the Atlantic, as cyclones over the Indian Ocean, and as typhoons over the Pacific. Whatever you like to call them, they bring big trouble!

BIRTH OF A KILLER

Hurricanes are born out at sea where the air is warmer than the surface of the ocean. Once storm clouds have massed, they start to spin. A hurricane can be almost 1,000 km across and contain hundreds of thunderstorms! These spiralling clouds are monitored by space satellites, but even with advance warnings, hurricanes still do tremendous damage.

Hurricane Fran, 1996

WHIRLING WINDS

Terrifying tornadoes and suffocating sandstorms - winds can cause as much trouble inland as hurricanes do along the coast. Although most tornadoes tear along at just 50 km/h, the winds inside them have been estimated at 800 km/h! Problem is, tornadoes are so fierce that they break all the measuring equipment!

Texan Tornado

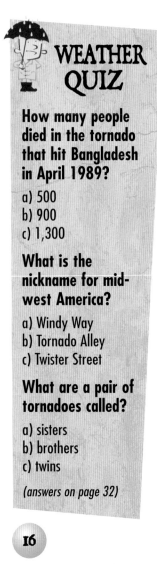

WEATHER QUIZ

How many people died in the tornado that hit Bangladesh in April 1989?

a) 500
b) 900
c) 1,300

What is the nickname for mid-west America?

a) Windy Way
b) Tornado Alley
c) Twister Street

What are a pair of tornadoes called?

a) sisters
b) brothers
c) twins

(answers on page 32)

SCHOOL'S OUT!

One of the luckiest escapes from tornado terror came in 1986 when 13 schoolchildren in China were safely set back down on the ground after being carried nearly 20 km through the air. As if that wasn't amazing enough, the wicked wind also managed to destroy the children's school! Now, who said 13 was unlucky?

VIOLENT VORTEX

So, where do tornadoes come from? Like hurricanes, they start life in a thundercloud which has built up over a hot day. Then a stubby funnel of cloud begins to spiral downwards. Once this twisting tube of air reaches the ground, it has become a full-blown and unstoppable tornado.

EGGS-ITING DISCOVERY

WHAT A CARRY-ON

When a tornado starts throwing its weight around, there's no telling what else it will throw! In the 1930s, a tornado in Minnesota actually tossed a train carriage about 8 metres through the air.

Millions of years ago in central Asia, sandstorms in the Gobi Desert buried whole packs of dinosaurs alive. The hot sand kept huge dinosaur eggs perfectly preserved.

DESERT STORM

The sphinx

Wild winds and desert sands make a deadly combination, aptly named the dust devil. Sand blows around in the air with enough force to strip paint off a car! For centuries, the ancient Egyptian pyramids and sphinx at Giza were completely buried under metres of sand dumped there by sandstorms.

FREAK FLOODS

Flash floods even happen in deserts. In fact, more people drown in deserts in the United States than die of thirst. Weird!

Monsoon floods, India

WEATHER QUIZ

What is the nickname of the Huang Ho River?

a) Stream of Sighs
b) Death River
c) China's Sorrow

Which place on Earth has most rainfall each year?

a) Mawsynram, India
b) Bognor Regis, England
c) Mount Rainier, United States

How do trees prevent floods?

a) their roots suck up rainwater
b) their roots bind the earth together
c) the leaves act as an umbrella

(answers on page 32)

WATER TORTURE

In 1998, China's longest river, the Yangtze became hell on Earth. Heavy rains flooded the river and 3,000 people died. Experts reckon the flooding was especially bad because people had chopped down the trees that had supported the river bank. Poor China also suffered the worst-ever flood. When the Huang Ho overflowed in 1887, nearly a million people lost their lives.

OH NOAH!

Could Noah's legendary flood have been real? Experts say there really was an enormous flood about 7,000 years ago. It had the force of about 200 Niagara Falls all put together.

RAIN... AGAIN!

Believe it or not, floods kill more people each year than all the other natural disasters in the world put together. Most floods happen when rivers burst their banks after filling up with water from torrential rains or melting snow.

WHAT A WASH-OUT

In the tropics, people depend on the annual rains. In places such as India and Bangladesh farmers need the precious water for their crops of rice and tea. But sometimes the monsoon winds bring too much rain. When the monsoons hit Thailand in 1983, 10,000 people lost their lives. As a result of drinking contaminated water, 100,000 people caught dangerous diseases.

Green frog

FLOOD OF FROGS?

It's not only rain that falls from the sky. Sometimes fierce winds, such as tornadoes, pick up animals, hurl them through the air, and drop them kilometres away. That might explain why there have been showers of fishes, frogs, rats, and even pigs!

WEATHER QUIZ

Where is the driest place in the world?

a) Bahrain
b) Sahara Desert, Africa
c) Atacama Desert, Chile

Which plant seeds need to be scorched by fire before they will start to grow?

a) phoenix fir
b) banksia shrub
c) tinder tree

Eucalyptus trees burn well in a bushfire. Why?

a) they contain flammable oil
b) their bark is very dry
c) their leaves contain no water

(answers on page 32)

DEATH IN THE DESERT

A scary skull is often all that remains of an animal after a drought. Once all the grass has died and the water supply dried up, many wild creatures become weak and die. But the vultures have a feast.

Steer's skull

FANNING THE FLAMES

As the plants wither and become tinder dry, the scene is set for wild fires. These are common in California, parts of Australia and in southern France. Sometimes a lightning bolt sets off the fire but more often it's human carelessness. Hot, dry winds fan the flames. A drought across the United States in 1988 left the whole of Yellowstone Park ablaze. Yikes, Yogi!

Yellowstone fire, 1988

FLAMES & FAMINE

You may think torrential rain causes problems – and it does – but things can also get pretty desperate when the rain fails to fall.

HIGH & DRY

Most wicked weather is over quite quickly, but droughts go on and on. In places like the Sahel in Africa, there has been a long-term drought for over 30 years. And the Atacama Desert in Chile once went without any rain for 400 years!

WHAT'S COOKING?

The highest temperature ever recorded was in Libya, North Africa. The temperature was 58°C in the shade – hot enough to fry an egg!

SMOKE & COUGHS

During 1997 and 1998, Southeast Asia suffered its deadliest drought in 50 years. It was so dry, whole forests caught fire. To make matters worse, the annual monsoon rains never came to put out the flames. For months, the fires raged out of control, choking the whole region with poisonous fumes.

PERFECT PRISM

One of the most glorious sights in the sky is the rainbow.
All sorts of myths surround this magnificent arch.

MYTH & MAGIC

Rainbow over France

For the ancient Greeks, a rainbow was the
path of the goddess Iris across the sky.
It was said to be God's promise to
Noah after the flood. And many
tribes – from the Masai of East
Africa to the Yuki of North
America – considered the
rainbow to be the robe of god.

COLOUR THEORY

The rainbow's colours are
always the same. From the
outside in they are red, orange,
yellow, green, blue, indigo and
violet. Remember them by taking
the first letters of this saying:
Richard of York gave battle in vain.

SEEING DOUBLE

Sometimes, two (or three) rainbows appear in
the sky. The outer one is usually the least bright and, unlike the main
rainbow, it is red on the inside and violet on the outside edge.

OVER THE RAINBOW

Most of the classic film *The Wizard of Oz* was set somewhere beyond the rainbow. The weather played a starring role as it was a raging tornado that carried Dorothy and her dog, Toto, into the land of Oz. Since rainbows are only visible when you are between the Sun and a rain shower, it's not really possible to go to the other side of a rainbow.

Scene from *The Wizard of Oz*

FLYING HIGH

If you're lucky enough to ever see a rainbow from the window of an aeroplane, you'll see something even more amazing than the Munchkins of Oz. Instead of appearing as a semicircular arch of colour, the rainbow makes a full circle!

GLITTERING PRIZE

According to legend, at the foot of a rainbow you'll find a crock of gold. Easy money? Sadly, rainbows never seem to touch the ground!

WEATHER QUIZ

What is a rainbow at night called?

a) a starbow
b) a moonbow
c) a nightbow

How long did the longest-lasting rainbow last?

a) about an hour
b) over six hours
c) five days

What type of 'rainbow' is colourless?

a) a fogbow
b) a whitebow
c) a palebow

(answers on page 32)

HELLO, HALO

If you thought only angels wore haloes, think again! Sometimes, a thin, white ring like a halo appears around the Sun or the Moon. It happens when light bounces off ice crystals that are falling through the air. A similar effect is a corona. This is a fuzzy circle of rainbow-coloured light seen encircling the Sun or Moon. But a corona is caused when light bounces off drops of rain, not crystals of ice.

WEATHER QUIZ

What is it called (apart from eclipse) when the Sun, Moon and Earth are positioned in a line?

a) hat trick
b) syzygy
c) lunasolterre

What are the most eclipses ever to have happened in a single year?

a) three
b) five
c) seven

Who was Aurora?

a) goddess of the dawn
b) an Inuit princess
c) first scientist to explain the northern lights

(answers on page 32)

TOTALLY AWESOME

Eclipses are one of the weirdest phenomena to experience. A solar eclipse happens when the Moon's path places it in front of the Sun, blocking its light from the Earth for several minutes. A spooky wind often blows as the temperature drops very sharply. The sky darkens and flowers shut their petals as if it is night. A solar eclipse can last up to about seven-and-a-half minutes.

SEEING TRIPLE

Mock suns, or sun dogs, are two bright points of light that appear either side of the real Sun. Sometimes, but only very rarely, the same effect happens at night and moon dogs are produced. Like haloes, sun and moon dogs are produced by light passing through ice crystals.

SPECIAL FX

Rainbows aren't the only stunning effects that the weather lays on for us. There are all sorts of tricks of the light that create some of the most wonderful sights on Earth.

QUANTUM PHYSICS

Auroras are extraordinary splashes of trembling colour that light up the night sky around the North and South Poles. *Aurora borealis*, also known as the northern lights, appear in the far north and *aurora australis* in the south. Auroras happen when particles called electrons from the Sun crash into particles of gas in the Earth's atmosphere. This spectacular display of coloured light is called a quantum.

Aurora borealis

REAL-LIFE GIANTS

A special effect called the Brocken Spectre creates scary giants in the sky! It happens when the Sun projects the shadows of people on a hilltop onto a nearby cloud.

WEATHER QUIZ

How far does sunlight have to travel to reach us?

a) 25,000 km
b) 150 million km
c) 15 billion km

Where were windmills invented?

a) in Persia (now Iran)
b) in Gaul (now France)
c) in the bath

What is the science boffin's name for a solar cell?

a) there isn't one
b) solarus cellus
c) a photovoltaic cell

(answers on page 32)

PUMP POWER

Windmills have been used for hundreds of years to grind grain or pump up water from below the ground. Today, there are about 250,000 of them around the world. Some still pump water but there are also high-tech turbines used to convert wind power into electricity.

SOLAR SPEEDSTER

Energy from the Sun (solar power) can be converted into electricity and used to run everything from pocket calculators to racing cars. The fastest car ever to have relied on Sun power alone is called *Sunraycer*. In June 1988 it achieved a speed of 78.39 km/h – a record that is still to be beaten.

GUSTS A GO-GO

Wind lends a helping hand when you're going places. The first sails on boats were probably made from animal skins but by the time of those crafty ancient Egyptians, people were using billowing sails of cloth. Today, some huge ocean liners have sails as well as engines. When the weather's windy, the captain cuts off the power and saves precious fuel. And of course, lots of people have fun using wind to power surfboards and yachts.

Windsurfer

WONDERFUL WEATHER

Come wind, rain, or shine, weather can be put to all sorts of good uses - including simply making us happy.
Best of all, it's free!

Sunraycer

DREAM ON

Many solar-powered vehicles carry back-up energy. Honda's *Dream Solar* car uses solar power for the first 90 km then switches over to a zinc battery that carries it another 100 km. The car holds the World Solar Challenge title, with an average speed of 85 km/h.

HOW SAD

It's scientifically proven - sunshine is good for you and a lack of it is bad. In winter, some people feel less happy than usual. Scientists reckon that because they are not getting enough light they may be suffering from Seasonal Affective Disorder (SAD).

THE ESSENTIALS

At a weather station, there is usually a wind vane that works out the direction of the prevailing (strongest) wind. Air temperature is measured by a thermometer. Scientists also measure how humid the air is (how much moisture it contains) and how much rain has fallen. But, most importantly of all, meteorologists must watch the sky to see what type of clouds are forming.

TORNADO TRAIL

Stormchasers aren't *all* weather scientists. Some loonies chase the deadliest storms on Earth – for fun!

WEATHER QUIZ

When was the first weather bulletin broadcast on radio?

a) 1922
b) 1933
c) 1944

Who made the first barometer?

a) Evangelista Torricelli
b) Galileo Galilei
c) Isaac Newton

What metallic element is used in thermometers?

a) quicksilver (mercury)
b) a heating element
c) glass

(answers on page 32)

Weather station

WEATHER WATCHERS

Forecasters gather all sorts of information to understand what the weather is going to do. They rely on weather stations dotted all over the planet, and weather balloons take readings from high in the atmosphere. Higher still, in space, satellites send back more information. All this data is fed into number-crunching supercomputers with enough processing power to make sense of it all.

WEATHER WHIZZ KIDS

OK, so weather forecasters often get it wrong, but what would we do without them? Meteorologists help ships and planes avoid serious storms and their forecasts allow farmers to plan when to plant and harvest their crops.

ANY WAY THE WIND BLOWS

Francis Beaufort knew the importance of observation. He was an admiral in the British Navy in the nineteenth century. He worked out a scale that would help sailors at sea to guess wind speed just by looking at its effects on the ocean. The scale goes from Force 1, when the air is still, to Force 12, which is a full-blown hurricane.

Weathercock

THE PRESSURE'S ON

Early weather scientists spent a lot of time finding out about air. Before they did anything else, it had to be proved that air even existed. After all, no one could see it! By the 1600s, scientists had discovered that air pressure affected the weather. High pressure meant that dry, stable weather was likely, whereas a sharp drop in pressure meant wind, rain and storms were on the way.

WEATHER QUIZ

What was the name of the first weather satellite?

a) *Telstar*
b) *Tiros 1*
c) *Rosti 1*

When were the first automated weather balloons launched?

a) 1798
b) 1898
c) 1918

What does WWW stand for?

a) Wild Wombat Wrestling
b) Web of Weather Watchers
c) World Weather Watch

(answers on page 32)

SPIES IN THE SKY

Since the **1960s**, satellites in space have been constantly taking photographs of the Earth. Weather satellites provide meteorologists with an overview of the clouds they simply cannot see from down here on Earth.

BUSY BALLOONS

Hundreds of huge, silvery weather balloons are released into the sky twice a day. Filled with helium, they rise slowly into the upper atmosphere. On board, robotic instruments take vital readings of the air's humidity and temperature, and air pressure. The results are transmitted back to special radio dishes on the ground. This wasn't always the case. In the early days, brave scientists went ballooning up to dizzying heights to study the skies.

Meteorologist with weather balloon

SAT STILL?

Weather satellites come in two types. Some always stay above the same spot and are called geostationary satellites. Others circle the globe from Pole to Pole. These are called polar-orbiting satellites.

Meteosat satellite

SAVING LIVES

Satellite views of storms have made it possible to predict the likely path of a hurricane. Armed with such information, governments can forewarn people in dangerous hurricane zones and try to evacuate them. In 1992, millions of people in the Bahamas and the USA were evacuated before the arrival of the extremely powerful Hurricane Andrew. Although 54 people still died, without the warnings it could have been thousands more.

SIZING UP

When you see pictures of satellites in space, they seem to be really huge. In fact, most are no bigger than an adult!

31

Index

Quiz answers

- **Page 2** c, Indra; b, Huracan; c, bullroarer.
- **Page 4** c, as the temperature rises; a, to forecast the weather – it swells and feels damp when rain is on the way; a, at night.
- **Page 7** b, contrail; a, mammatus (breast); c, mackerel sky.
- **Page 8** a, Jack Frost; a, over 90 per cent; b, the *Titanic*.
- **Page 10** c, Vostok, Antarctica; a,b,c, trick question – eyeballs, petrol, and the sea will all freeze; b, 150.
- **Page 13** c, lightning usually strikes tall objects; c, 500 times a year; a, Benjamin Franklin.
- **Page 14** a, eye; b, more than 119 km/h; a, swell of seawater.

- **Page 16** c, 1,300; b, Tornado Alley; a, sisters.
- **Page 18** c, China's Sorrow; a, Mawsynram, India; a, b, trick question – roots suck up rainwater and bind the earth together.
- **Page 20** c, Atacama Desert, Chile; b, banksia shrub; a, they contain flammable oil.
- **Page 23** b, moonbow; b, over six hours; a, fogbow.
- **Page 24** b, syzygy; c, seven; a, goddess of the dawn.
- **Page 26** b, 150 million km; a, in Persia (now Iran); c, a photovoltaic cell.
- **Page 28** a, 1922; a, Evangelista Torricelli; a, quicksilver (mercury).
- **Page 30** b, *Tiros 1*; b, 1898; c, World Weather Watch.

Acknowledgements

Copyright © 2006 **ticktock** Entertainment Ltd. First published in Great Britain by ticktock Media Ltd.,
Unit 2, Orchard Business Centre, North Farm Road, Tunbridge Wells, Kent TN2 3XF, Great Britain.
A CIP catalogue record for this book is available from the British Library.
ISBN 1 86007 953 9 Printed in China.

Picture Credits: t = top, b = bottom, c = centre, l = left, r=right, OFC = outside front cover, OBC = outside back cover, IFC = inside front cover
Corbis; 2tl. Gamma; 10/11t, 14/15t, 20bl. Oxford Scientific Films; 4/5c, 5b, 10/11b. Ronald Grant Archive; 12bl, 23tr. Science Photo Library; 8tl, 15br, 25cr, 26/27t, 28c, 30/31bc, 31tr. Tony Stone Images; OFC (main picture), 2/3c, 6/7c, 7tr, 8/9, 12/13c, 16/17c, 17br, 18/19t, 19br, 20/21c, 22c, 24/25t, 26bl.